Nibble
MANIA ®

Cathy Prange and Joan Pauli

Macmillan Canada
Toronto

Nibble Mania®
by Cathy Prange and Joan Pauli
Copyright © 1983, 1998

Canadian Cataloguing in Publication Data

Prange, Cathy, 1931–
Nibble mania

ISBN 0-7715-7557-2

1. Appetizers.   2. Snack foods.   I. Pauli, Joan, 1937–   . II. Title

TX740.P733 1998   641.8'12   C97-932158-1

1 2 3 4 5 TRI 02 01 00 99 98

This book is available at special discounts for bulk purchases by your group or organization for sales promotions, premiums, fundraising and seminars. For details, contact: Macmillan Canada, Special Sales Department, 29 Birch Avenue, Toronto, ON M4V 1E2. Tel: 416-963-8830.

Pictured on cover:
Louise's Crab Stuffed Snow Peas, 62
Mini Pizza, 20
Donna's Shrimp Mousse, 60

Photography: Hal Roth
Photo Assistant: Andrew Tomkins
Food Stylist: Lasha Andrushko

Macmillan Canada
A Division of Canada Publishing Corporation
Toronto, Ontario, Canada

Printed in Canada

NIBBLE MANIA

MANY FRIDAY MORNINGS have come and gone through our kitchens since *Muffin Mania* first hit the book shelves–and yes, we are still baking those scrumptious muffins. However, not quite as often as before, as our families are quick to point out. As a matter of fact, we've been forced to alter our daily cooking pattern in order to respond to the tremendous support you have given us for *Muffin Mania*.

Many were the nights that the meals consisted of finger food, simple snacks, appetizers, or whatever you want to call them, and before we knew it, we found ourselves right in the middle of a brand new craze, or mania, which we now want to share with you. As you'll find out, *Nibble Mania* can be as much fun as *Muffin Mania*!

Nibbles are so simple and so easy to make. They're scrumptious and nutritious to eat–our families and nibble-tasting gal friends can vouch for that! Once again we called upon their taste buds and endorsements to be sure we offered you only the best recipes. Their encouragement has convinced us to share our very favourite, well-tested recipes with you.

You don't have to put away your muffin tins! They can be used for several of our recipes. These easy nibbles can be made ahead, frozen, and heated as needed at a later date–ideal if friends drop in for dinner, lunch, a party or just a drink. It's nice to be prepared and you'll be an instant hit! They are also great for a quiet evening at home or at the cottage by candle-light or in front of the fireplace.

So gals, and all you guys who love to cook, we're sure you'll find a nifty nibble to suit almost any occasion, and the best part is, you can relax and enjoy too!

Have fun and good tasting!

Sisters, Partners and Yes,
Still Friends,
Cathy Prange
Joan Pauli

HINTS

Have everything ready,
Before guests are due.
You'll enjoy yourself more,
And they will too!

1. When serving nibbles as an "appeteaser" before dinner, limit them to four kinds as they should stimulate the appetite rather than satisfy.

2. Whichever you choose to serve, keep your tray simple and uncluttered. Make interesting combinations as to colour and taste.

3. If freezing and reheating, wrap in foil to prevent drying. Bake at 300° F for 10 min. if thawed, or until hot.

4. Those made in muffin cups may be served for lunch by using tins with larger cups and not separating biscuits. The fillings may also be put into toast cups, bouchées made with puff pastry or tart shells.

5. Cheese balls may be kept for several days in the refrigerator. Freeze for longer storage. To freeze cheese balls, wrap in plastic wrap or foil. Thaw in refrigerator.

6. For easy unmolding of mousses, grease mold first and put in freezer while preparing the mousse.

7. For variety and time-saving, get together with friends and exchange your nifty nibbles.

CONTENTS

Nibbles

Hot Stuff

Say Cheese

Dips and Spreads

Hooked on Seafood

Nibbles

Celery Seed Bread

---

  1 loaf french bread, unsliced
  ½ c. butter, softened
  1 tsp. celery or poppy seed
  ¼ tsp. salt
  ¼ tsp. paprika
  Dash cayenne

Cutting bread nearly to bottom, make 1-inch slices in
the loaf.

Mix all ingredients and spread mixture in and out of every
slice and ice the top with leftover.

Place buttered loaf on baking sheet.

Cover with waxed paper and chill.

Uncover and bake at 400° F for 15–20 min. or until golden.

To make spreading easier, melt butter and add seasonings and
brush the sections. We sometimes double the mixture so we
have lots to ice the top.

*This recipe will bring raves and is a nice change from
garlic bread.*

Cheese Snacks

---

1 c. grated sharp cheddar cheese
1 c. crushed potato chips
¼ c. butter, softened
½ c. flour
1 tsp. prepared mustard

Blend all ingredients and drop from teaspoon on ungreased cookie sheet.

Flatten with the back of a spoon and bake at 375° F for 5–8 min.

Store in tins. Keep in refrigerator.

May be frozen.

These are a delicious nibble served hot or cold.

Cheese Wafers

---

1 pkg. Imperial cheese, softened
   (the kind in the flat, round container)
½ c. corn oil
1 c. flour
3 tsp. worcestershire sauce
Dash cayenne
2 c. Rice Krispies

Mix together cheese, oil, flour, worcestershire and cayenne.

Stir in Rice Krispies.

Form into small balls. Place on cookie sheet and flatten with a fork which has been dipped into cold water.

Bake at 325° F for 10–12 min. or until golden. Store in tins in refrigerator.

May be frozen.

These are good served hot or cold.

Why not add ½ c. crumbled bacon or bacon bits to these? M-m-m good!

Helen's Cheese Shortbread

1 c. butter, softened
2 c. grated sharp cheese
2 c. flour
1 tsp. salt

Cream butter and cheese. Mix in flour and salt. Chill.

Cut in shapes and bake at 350° F for 12 min. or until slightly browned.

Or

Mold into two rolls, 1 inch in diameter. (Dough may be soft, but not to worry!)

Wrap in wax paper and refrigerate two hours or overnight.

Cut into ¼-inch slices and bake as above.

Serve hot!

Delicious any time of the day—or night.

Nuts and Bolts

---

1 lb. salted mixed nuts
½ lb. cashews
½ lb. peanuts
1 box Shreddies
1 box Cheerios
1 pkg. (8 oz.) pretzel sticks, cut in half
2 c. peanut oil or 1 c. butter, softened,
    and 1 c. peanut oil
2 tbsp. worcestershire sauce
1 tbsp. garlic salt
1 tbsp. seasoned salt
1 tsp. celery salt

In large roasting pan, combine first six ingredients.

Mix remaining ingredients together and pour over mixture in pan.

Bake at 200° F for 2 hrs. Stir frequently.

Pack into jars or freeze in freezer bags.

This recipe makes a very large quantity, so it may easily be cut in half.

Nice to pack in jars as gifts at Christmastime.

Oriental Munch

½ c. butter
4 tbsp. soya sauce
2 tsp. seasoned salt
2 tsp. worcestershire sauce
1 tsp. Tabasco sauce
½ tsp. garlic powder
2 c. chow mein noodles
2 c. pretzel sticks, halved
2 c. Shreddies
2 c. Riceroos
1 c. pecans
1 c. cashews

Melt butter and stir in the next five ingredients (seasonings).

Place remaining ingredients in roasting pan and pour butter mixture over. Toss lightly to blend.

Place in oven at 200° F for 1 hr., stirring occasionally.

Pack into jars. "Yummy."

If you can't find Riceroos, Rice Chex or Cheerios may be substituted.

A great nibble for your bridge table, but have the drinks ready!

Spicy Bread Sticks

½ c. butter
½ tsp. garlic salt
½ tsp. celery salt
½ tsp. seasoned salt
1-½ tbsp. worcestershire sauce
2 dashes Tabasco sauce
2 pkg. bread sticks

Heat oven to 300° F.

Put butter in roasting pan and heat until melted.
Remove pan from oven and stir in seasoning.

Roll sticks until coated on all sides. Spread out on cookie
sheet and heat 20 min.

Turn several times, then turn oven off and leave in until
crispy and dry.

Will keep in covered tin.

A fun finger food to serve with soups, salads and dips.

Auntie Thelma's Almond Toffee

¾ c. butter
1 c. white sugar (she uses ¾ c.)
1 c. whole unblanched almonds
½ c. chocolate chips
⅓ c. crushed pecans

Melt butter over low heat.

Add sugar. Stir gently and just before it boils add almonds.

Boil moderately (stirring) until very hard when tested in cold water, about 10–15 min.

Pour quickly into an ungreased cookie sheet, spreading almonds evenly.

Spread scant layer of chocolate chips on top of toffee and let melt.

Spread carefully over toffee.

Sprinkle pecans on top.

Put in refrigerator until hard.

Break into small pieces with fingers and place in refrigerator in a tin.

Without a doubt, the best candy our families have ever tasted! Our Christmas would not be complete without receiving our box from Auntie Thelma.

Candied Nuts

---

2 c. peanuts (without skins)
½ c. white sugar
2 tbsp. butter
1 tsp. vanilla
¾ tsp. salt

In large frypan, heat nuts, sugar and butter over medium heat, stirring constantly, until golden brown–about 15 min.

Remove from heat and stir in vanilla.

Spread mixture on lightly buttered cookie sheet. Sprinkle with salt. (If salted peanuts are used, omit salt.)

Cool and break into clusters.

These are especially good when whole unblanched almonds are used.

Pack these marvelous munchies in pretty jars to give to friends before your family tastes them!

Chocolate Clusters

1 pkg. (6 oz.) chocolate chips
1 pkg. (6 oz.) butterscotch chips
1 c. chow mein noodles
1 c. peanuts

Melt chocolate and butterscotch chips together. Stir in noodles and peanuts.

Drop by teaspoon on waxed paper and cool.

Store in tins in refrigerator.

Cornflake Nibblers

---

2 pkg. (6 oz. each) butterscotch chips
½ c. peanut butter
6 c. cornflakes

Melt chips and peanut butter together in large saucepan over low heat.

Add cornflakes and mix well.

Drop by large teaspoon on waxed paper.

Refrigerate for several hours.

Put in tin and store in refrigerator.

Both these treats may be frozen in plastic bags. A colourful addition to your Christmas cookie tray.

Hot Stuff

Blue Cheese Bites

1 pkg. refrigerator biscuits
¼ c. butter
4 oz. blue cheese

Cut each biscuit in quarters and arrange in a baking dish.

Melt cheese and butter together.

Pour over biscuits, coating well.

Bake at 400° F for 12–15 min.

Makes 40.

These would also be delicious using cheddar or any other kind of cheese.

What could be easier than this quick appeteaser for the working gal or guy?

Cocktail Meatballs in Barbeque Sauce

2 lbs. lean ground beef
1 egg
1 pkg. onion soup mix (dry)
2 tsp. Accent
¼ c. dry bread crumbs

Mix together and form into 1-inch balls and brown.

Barbeque Sauce
1 pkg. spaghetti sauce mix (dry)
2 small jars red currant jelly
2 small bottles ketchup

Put all ingredients in saucepan and simmer 40 min.

Add meatballs and heat through. Serve with cocktail picks.

Meatballs may be frozen in plastic bags after browning and added to sauce when needed.

Eat sparingly—almost a meal in itself!

Duncan's Chicken Wings
(Sweet & Sour)

2 lbs. chicken wings
2 tbsp. wine vinegar
4 tbsp. oil
2 tbsp. soya sauce
2 large garlic cloves, crushed
2 tbsp. orange marmalade
2 tbsp. honey
1 tbsp. lemon juice

Wash chicken wings, cut in half at joint and discard tips.

Combine sauce ingredients in a large baking dish.

Place wings in dish, turning well to coat each wing, and allow to marinate for one hour or more, turning several times to coat.

Bake uncovered in 350° F oven for approx. 1 hr., turning wings occasionally to baste.

These wings are delicious hot or cold, or served with Blue Cheese Dip (see page 43).

Hot Spinach Balls

2 pkg. (10 oz. each) frozen spinach,
   cooked and drained very well
2 c. packaged stuffing mix
1 c. grated parmesan cheese
6 eggs, beaten
¾ c. butter, softened
1 tbsp. garlic salt
½ tsp. Accent
½ tsp. pepper
½ tsp. thyme

Combine all ingredients, mixing well.

Roll into balls about the size of a walnut. Put on cookie sheet and freeze. When frozen, put in freezer bags.

Bake from frozen state at 350° F for 10–15 min.

These are quite gooey before baking, but don't fret.
They are moist and delicious for those who like spinach.

Julia's Cheese Things

---

1 pkg. refrigerator crescent rolls
4 tbsp. butter, softened
3 eggs, beaten
1 c. broken salad olives
1 onion, chopped
4 c. grated sharp cheddar cheese
Dash cayenne

Unwrap crescent rolls and pat into 9 x 15-inch pan, smoothing out the seams.

Mix all the ingredients and pour over dough.

Bake at 350° F for 15–20 min. or until set.

Cool and cut in squares and put on cookie sheet to freeze. When frozen, put in freezer bags.

This is one of our favourites for family fun or formal functions!

Olive Cheese Balls

¼ c. butter, softened
1 c. grated sharp cheddar cheese (4 oz.)
½ c. flour
¼ tsp. salt
½ tsp. paprika
24 small stuffed olives

In small bowl, blend together butter and cheese. Stir in flour, salt and paprika and mix well.

Dry olives on paper towel. Mold dough around olives, covering completely.

Bake at 400° F for 10 min. or until golden.

May be frozen and reheated in foil at 325° F for 5 min. These may also be frozen before baking and kept up to 2 months.

Variation:
This dough may be molded around a date, pecan or dill pickle, or add ¼ c. salad olives to the dough and form into small balls, sprinkle with paprika and bake.

Mini Pizza

---

2 pkg. (8 oz. each) cans refrigerator butterflake rolls
1 jar or can thick spaghetti sauce
Chopped olives, mushrooms or whatever
Grated parmesan or mozzarella cheese

Separate each roll in two and flatten on cookie sheet. Bake for 5 min. at 350° F.

Remove from oven and make indent with back of spoon.

Spoon on sauce and toppings of your choice.

Top with cheese and bake at 350° F for 10–15 min. or until cheese bubbles.

These pizzas can be cooled and frozen.

Mini Quiches

---

2 pkg. (8 oz. each) refrigerator butterflake rolls
1 can sliced mushrooms, drained
1 egg, beaten
½ c. sour cream
1 tbsp. sherry
½ tsp. salt
Dash pepper
Gruyère or swiss cheese

Spray or grease small muffin tins. Separate each biscuit into two and press into tins. Place small amount of mushrooms in each.

Combine egg, sour cream and seasonings and pour a spoonful on top of the mushrooms. Cut cheese in small pieces and place on top.

Bake at 350° F for 10–15 min.

Cool and freeze.

To reheat, wrap in foil and bake at 300° F for 10 min.

This recipe makes 40 appeteasers.

Variation:
Instead of mushrooms, use small shrimp (1 can shrimp, drained, or 1 can flaked crab meat).

Or

Get together with a friend and exchange.

Mother Milner's Old-Fashioned Bacon Strips

Trim crusts from sliced bread.

Butter bread lightly and spread with nippy cheese.

Brush tops with slightly beaten egg white.

Cut bacon in small strips and place on top.

Bake at 400° F until bacon is cooked.

Cut in quarters and serve hot.

Mother used to make these for Bridge Club, and as kids we hoped for leftovers to eat cold for breakfast.

Another Oldie But Goodie

Spread condensed cream of mushroom soup on bread slices (crusts removed).

Roll like a jelly roll.

Secure with toothpick and bake at 350° F until bread is toasted.

These could be cut in half for a nibble or left whole for a snack.

Mushroom Caps

---

20 large mushrooms
2 medium-sized onions
2 tbsp. butter
4 oz. cream cheese, softened
Italian dressing mix (dry)
Dash Accent
Dash cayenne

Chop mushroom stems and onions finely, and sauté in butter until onions are transparent.

Mix with softened cream cheese and fill mushroom caps.

Sprinkle with italian dressing mix, a touch of Accent and a dash of cayenne.

Bake at 350° F for 10 min., then broil until slightly brown.

Delicious and different—easily eaten with the fingers.

Stuffed Mushroom Caps

½ c. butter
1 tbsp. garlic powder
1 tsp. lemon juice
1-½ c. parmesan cheese (approx.)

Melt butter.

Add garlic powder, lemon juice and parmesan cheese.

You may add finely chopped mushroom stems or ½ c. dry bread crumbs at this point if desired.

Fill mushroom caps and place in baking dish.

Bake at 350° F for 10 min., then broil until nicely browned.

Variation:
Before baking, top with an escargot and baste with the melted butter from your pan.

Party Toasted Cheese Squares

1 lb. cheddar cheese grated (2 cups)
½ lb. butter, softened
1 tsp. dry mustard
1 tsp. worcestershire sauce
1 egg, well beaten
1 tbsp. grated onion
¼ tsp. pepper
2-3 drops Tabasco sauce
1 loaf sandwich bread, thinly sliced

Mix all ingredients except the bread and beat well.

Trim crusts from bread. Using two slices of bread at a time, spread mixture between slices, on top and on sides.

Cut sandwiches into 4 squares.

Place in refrigerator for several hours before baking.

Bake on lightly buttered pan at 325° F for 15 min. or until lightly browned.

Remove and serve hot.

Or, cool on pan and freeze in freezer bags for later use.

If you love cheese like we do, you'll always have a bag of these in your freezer! Bring them out to serve with lunch, for your cocktail hour or for your bed-time snack.

Roast Pig Tails

10 lb. box short pig tails
1 can (10 oz.) beef gravy (or freeze leftover gravy from
    beef, chicken or turkey and save for this recipe)
5 c. boiling water
3 tbsp. vinegar
6 tbsp. brown sugar
1 tsp. salt
1 tsp. Accent
½ tsp. pepper
1 tsp. garlic salt
3 tbsp. gravy improver
1 bottle beer

Trim fat from pig tails.

Mix all other ingredients.

Put pig tails in large roasting pan and pour sauce over.

Bake uncovered at 325° F for 3 hrs.

Baste every 20 min. During last hour of baking, pour in a
bottle of beer. This will cut the fat.

*A traditional Waterloo County meal served with sauerkraut
(with caraway) or as a nifty nibble.*

Sausage and Bacon Quiche

---

3 c. chopped onion
½ lb. bacon, cut in fine pieces
1 lb. sausage meat
1-½ c. sour cream
2 tbsp. flour
⅓ c. milk
½ tsp. salt
3 eggs, beaten
1 tsp. caraway seeds
1 pkg. refrigerator crescent rolls

Brown onion and bacon pieces. Drain off grease and set aside on paper towels.

Brown sausage meat and drain well. Stir in onion and bacon.

Blend sour cream with flour and stir in milk, salt, beaten eggs and caraway seeds.

Unroll crescent rolls and press in 9 x 15-inch pan, covering bottom and sides.

Spread bacon, onion and sausage mixture over dough.

Pour sour cream mixture on top.

Bake at 325° F for 40 min. or until filling is set. Cut into snack pieces and serve hot.

May be frozen. Put pieces on cookie sheet in freezer and when frozen, put in plastic bag.

This is also good with coffee for brunch.
Serve with Grandma Prange's Tomato Butter (page 48).

Savoury Snacks

½ lb. lean ground beef
¼ c. chopped onion
1 c. chopped celery
1 envelope Sloppy Joe mix (dry)
1 can (5-½ oz.) tomato paste
¾ c. water
2 tbsp. apple jelly or red currant jelly
1 pkg. (8 oz.) refrigerator butterflake rolls

Brown meat and onions. Add all other ingredients except butterflake rolls.

Divide each butterflake roll into two and press into small muffin tins. Put filling in and bake at 350° F for 15 min.

Cool and freeze.

If you are a cheese lover, top with your favourite cheese before baking.

This filling can be made ahead and put in jars and stored in the refrigerator.

Scotch Eggs

1 lb. sausage meat
6 hard-boiled eggs, shelled
¼ c. flour seasoned with salt and pepper to taste
2 eggs, beaten
¼ tsp. sage
¼ tsp. basil (optional)
Cracker crumbs
Oil for browning

Divide sausage meat into 6 portions. Flour hands and place a portion of sausage meat in palm. Place an egg in centre and work meat around.

Dip in flour, raw egg and crumbs. Fry on all sides in 1 inch hot oil.

Slice and serve hot as a finger food or serve whole with potato salad for lunch.

Turn this one into breakfast for guests, but don't forget Grandma Prange's Tomato Butter (page 48)!

Water Chestnuts Wrapped in Bacon

¼ c. oil
¼ c. soya sauce
2 tbsp. ketchup
1 tbsp. vinegar
Dash pepper
2 cloves garlic, crushed
2 cans water chestnuts, drained
1 lb. bacon, cut in half slices

Mix all ingredients except chestnuts and bacon.

Add chestnuts to sauce and marinate 4 hrs.

Wrap each chestnut in half slice of bacon and secure with toothpick.

Broil at 500° F for 8–10 min. or until bacon is done.
Serve hot.

Or cool and put in plastic bags and freeze for later use.

Variation:
Marinate chicken livers in sauce for 4 hrs. and wrap with bacon and broil.

Or sprinkle smoked oysters with lemon juice and wrap bacon half around two smoked oysters and broil.

Wilma's Glazed Sausage Bites

---

1 lb. bulk pork sausage
1 slightly beaten egg
½ c. cracker crumbs
½ tsp. sage

Combine above. Shape into 1-inch balls and brown slowly.
Don't brown in oil as these are quite gooey.

Sauce
¼ c. water
¼ c. ketchup
2 tbsp. brown sugar
1 tbsp. vinegar
1 tbsp. soya sauce

Combine sauce ingredients and pour over sausage balls.
Simmer 15 min. Stir occasionally. Serve with cocktail picks
or forks.

*Your men folk could make a meal of these, so make them for
dinner with rice!*

Say Cheese!

Dried Beef Log

1 pkg. (8 oz.) cream cheese, softened
1 tbsp. grated onion or onion flakes
¼ c. parmesan cheese
1 tbsp. horseradish
1 can (2-½ oz.) chipped beef

Blend together all except beef. Put in refrigerator to harden.

Chop beef finely.

Shape cheese in log and roll in chipped beef.

If you can't find chipped beef, flaked corned beef is just as good.

Ham and Pineapple Log

1 pkg. (8 oz.) cream cheese, softened
1 small can crushed pineapple, well drained
  on paper towels
¼ c. chopped green peppers
1 tbsp. finely chopped onion
1-½ tsp. seasoned salt
1 small can (4 oz.) devilled ham
1 c. chopped pecans

Mix all but nuts.

Refrigerate to harden.

Roll in pecans.

Freezer Cheese Balls

---

8 oz. sharp cheddar cheese, grated
1 pkg. (8 oz.) cream cheese, softened
4 oz. blue cheese
1 clove garlic, minced
¼ c. butter, softened
¾ c. chopped nuts, walnuts or pecans

Mix cheeses together.

Mix in garlic and butter.

Chill well and form into 4 balls and roll in chopped nuts.

May be frozen.

Ham and Cheese Ball

1 pkg. (8 oz.) cream cheese
¼ c. mayonnaise
2 cans (8 oz. each) flakes of ham
2 tbsp. chopped parsley
    or 3 tbsp. chopped salad olives or both
1 tsp. minced onion
¼ tsp. dry mustard
¼ tsp. Tabasco sauce
½ c. chopped nuts

Cream the cheese and mayonnaise until smooth. Stir in the next 5 ingredients.

Cover and chill several hours.

Mold into two balls and roll in chopped nuts.

Cheese balls may be frozen.

Nippy Corned Beef and Cheese Ball

---

1 small pkg. (4 oz.) cream cheese, softened
1 c. grated cheddar cheese
1 can (6 oz.) corned beef, shredded
1 tsp. horseradish
1 tsp. prepared mustard
¼ tsp. worcestershire sauce
¼ tsp. grated lemon rind
2 tbsp. lemon juice
⅓ c. sweet pickle relish, drained
½ c. parsley flakes

In a mixer bowl (or food processor) blend together thoroughly: cheeses, corned beef, horseradish, mustard, worcestershire sauce, lemon rind and juice and pickle relish.

Cover and refrigerate until firm.

Shape into two balls and roll in parsley.

Wrap and refrigerate or freeze.

Party Cheese Ball

---

1 lb. sharp cheddar cheese, grated
2 pkg. (8 oz. each) cream cheese, softened
½ c. chopped stuffed olives
¼ tsp. baking soda
¼ c. evaporated milk
½ tsp. Tabasco sauce
1 tbsp. parsley flakes
1 tbsp. grated onion or onion flakes
1 clove garlic, minced, or 1 tsp. garlic powder
1 tbsp. worcestershire sauce
1 tsp. lemon juice
1 c. chopped pecans

Combine cheeses and mix well. Add remaining ingredients except chopped pecans.

Refrigerate for 2–3 hrs.

Mold into two balls or two logs and roll in chopped nuts or add chopped pecans with the rest of ingredients and mold into two balls.

May be frozen.

Pineapple Cheese Balls

1 pkg. (4 oz.) cream cheese
¼ c. drained, crushed pineapple
¼ c. chopped nuts

Cream the cheese until smooth.

Add pineapple and blend.

Form into ½-inch balls and roll in chopped nuts.

Chill. At serving time, pierce each ball with a pretzel stick.

Yields 24 balls.

SAY CHEESE!

Pop's Potted Cheese

> 1 lb. sharp cheddar cheese, grated
> ¼ c. minced green onion tops
> 1 tbsp. dijon mustard
> 1 oz. cognac, brandy or dry sherry
> 2 tbsp. butter, softened
> Cream (optional)

Combine cheese and onion tops.

Gradually blend in mustard, cognac and butter.

Stir until smooth, adding more butter or cream to make it easy to spread.

Pack into small crocks and seal tightly with plastic wrap and store in refrigerator.

Serve at room temperature.

This is delicious on french bread or crackers with a soup or salad supper!

If you like curry, ½ tsp. curry powder added to this gives a nice flavour.

This improves with age—like Pop!

Sir Sam's Wheel of Brie

1 pkg. of brie cheese
2 tbsp. butter
1 tbsp. lemon juice
1 tsp. garlic powder
2 tbsp. unblanched almonds
Pumpernickel bread

Remove foil from cheese and place on oven-proof plate.

In small saucepan, melt butter; add lemon juice and garlic powder and stir.

Spoon butter mixture over cheese and put almonds on top.

Bake at 300° F for 20 min. or until almonds are brown and cheese is heated through.

Remove to round platter and cut pumpernickel bread into triangles and arrange around cheese to look like spokes of a wheel.

This is also good using camembert and nuts of your choice.

We shared this as an appetizer before dinner on a ski week-end at Sir Sam's in Haliburton. The chef was kind enough to give us his recipe. We found this dish too delicious to share.

Three Cheese Ball

4 oz. smoked cheese
4 oz. blue cheese
1 pkg. (8 oz.) cream cheese
1 tbsp. onion flakes
1 tsp. worcestershire sauce
2 tbsp. minced parsley
½ c. chopped pecans

Combine cheeses and beat until fluffy.

Beat in onion and worcestershire sauce.

Cover and chill in refrigerator overnight. Combine parsley and pecans.

Mold mixture into one large or two smaller balls and roll in parsley and nut mixture.

May be frozen.

Serve as spread with variety of crackers.

Dips and
Spreads

Blue Cheese Dip

1 c. mayonnaise
2 tbsp. finely chopped onion
1 tbsp. garlic powder
¼ c. finely chopped parsley
½ c. sour cream
1 tbsp. lemon juice
1 tbsp. vinegar
¼ c. blue cheese, crumbled
Salt (optional)
Freshly ground pepper
Dash cayenne

Combine all ingredients in a mixing bowl.

Refrigerate for at least 1 hr. **Yields 2-½ cups.**

Garlic Butter

½ lb. butter, softened
2 tbsp. chopped parsley
4-5 garlic cloves, minced
Freshly ground pepper
1 tbsp. onion flakes
½ tbsp. lemon juice

Mix all ingredients.

To store, roll in aluminum foil.

Will keep in refrigerator for 3 months.

Canapé Spreads

A

1 pkg. (8 oz.) cream cheese, softened
½ c. mayonnaise
½ c. finely chopped walnuts
1 small can crushed pineapple, drained

Blend all ingredients and chill.

B

2 c. ground cooked ham or flakes of ham
½ c. mayonnaise
2 hard-boiled eggs, chopped
¼ c. ground sweet pickles or drained pickle relish
2 tbsp. finely chopped onion.

Blend all ingredients and chill.

C

8 oz. cottage cheese
1 can flakes of chicken
3 tbsp. finely chopped onion
2 tbsp. parsley flakes
¼ tsp. garlic powder
¼ tsp. paprika

Blend all ingredients and chill.

Easy, make-ahead spreads for crunchy veggies and crackers.

Donna's Antipasto

½ small head cauliflower,
　　separated into tiny flowerettes
1 jar (8 oz.) olives with pimento, drained
1 jar (8 oz.) sweet pickled onions, drained
1 bottle (32 oz.) ketchup
3 green peppers, chopped
½ c. olive oil or corn oil
¼ c. vinegar
2 cans (7 oz. each) chunk tuna, drained
1 can sliced mushrooms, drained
1 can (7 oz.) small shrimp, drained
1 jar (14 oz.) pitted black olives, sliced
　　(optional–we leave out)

In large saucepan, pre-cook cauliflowerettes 5 min. and drain.
Add olives, onions, ketchup, peppers, oil and vinegar and
simmer gently 10 min.

Add tuna, mushrooms, shrimp and black olives, if using.
Simmer gently for 30 min.

Bottle and refrigerate.

This recipe makes about 2 quarts and keeps for ages.

Serve with rye bread or melba toast and crackers.

Simply scrumptious.

*This recipe takes a little more time, but makes a large quantity
and is well worth the effort.*

Frosted Liver Pâté

1 lb. liverwurst
3 tbsp. minced onion
1 clove garlic, crushed
½ tsp. basil, thyme and oregano

Mash liverwurst and mix in all other ingredients. Place on plate and shape into loaf with rounded top. Chill.

Cream Cheese Topping
1 pkg (8 oz.) cream cheese, softened
1 tsp. mayonnaise
1 clove garlic, minced
Dash Tabasco sauce

Mix all ingredients together and ice pâté. This may be decorated for party fun with parsley, etc.

Try shaping into a football for a Grey Cup party and make stripes with red pimento.

Glazed Braunschweiger Mousse

1 envelope unflavoured gelatin
¼ c. cold water
1 (10 oz.) consommé
½ lb. or 1 roll braunschweiger
3 tbsp. mayonnaise
½ onion, finley chopped
1 tsp. worcestershire sauce
1 tsp. vinegar
Dash pepper

Soften gelatin in cold water.

Heat consommé to boiling and add softened gelatin.

Put a thin layer in bottom of mold or individual molds. Chill.

Blend all other ingredients thoroughly.

Fill mold or molds with meat mixture and pour rest of consommé over.

Chill until firm.

Unmold and serve with rye bread and crackers. May be frozen.

For a nice change, try adding some brandy, sherry, nuts or olives to the meat mixture.

Grandma Prange's Tomato Butter

1 basket (6 qt.) basket ripe tomatoes
4 c. vinegar
1 small bag pickling spice
1 sweet red pepper, finely chopped
1-½ tbsp. salt
3 lbs. (6 c.) white sugar

Skin and slice tomatoes and let stand overnight.

Drain off water.

To pulp, add the vinegar and boil until soft.

Add bag of pickling spice and the red pepper and salt.

Boil 1 hr., then add sugar and boil until thick, at least 3 hrs.

Stir often to prevent burning.

Pour into sterilized jars. Makes about 4–6 pts.

Tomato Butter is super with bacon and eggs and all meats for dinner. We love to put it on a slice of tomato.

Homemade Mayonnaise

¾ c. white sugar
1-½ tsp. salt
1-½ tsp. cornstarch
2 tsp. mustard
¾ c. vinegar
2 eggs
1 tbsp. butter

Mix sugar, salt, cornstarch and mustard together.

Gradually add vinegar and bring to a boil.

Beat eggs, add small amount of hot mixture to eggs first and then add all the egg mixture to the hot mixture and boil again until thickened.

Remove from heat and add butter. Pour in jar.

A sweet mayonnaise for sandwich fillings and devilled eggs.

Mildred's Chicken Liver Pâté

    1 lb. chicken livers
    1 c. butter
    1 medium onion, sliced
    ½ tsp. curry powder
    ½ tsp. paprika
    ¼ tsp. salt
    ⅛ tsp. pepper
    1–2 cloves garlic, crushed

Trim any fat off chicken livers.

Melt the butter and cook the chicken livers, onion and seasonings in butter over medium heat until onions are soft.

Blend in blender or food processor a small amount at a time until smooth.

Pour in mold or loaf pan and chill overnight. Serve with Triscuits or melba toast.

Even our non-liver-lover friends enjoyed this tasty and simple recipe.

Mrs. Scott's Mustard

1 c. brown sugar
⅓ c. dry mustard
2 eggs
⅓ c. cider vinegar
2 tbsp. butter

Mix together the brown sugar, dry mustard, eggs, and vinegar. Cook until thick.

Remove from heat and add the butter. Store in jar.

This is a yummy sweet mustard—not too hot. Good as a dip for cocktail sausages or sausage balls. A must at Oktoberfest with ham and roast pork.

Mrs. Scott's Seafood Sauce

2 oz. malt vinegar
⅛ tsp. salt
½ tsp. worcestershire sauce
½ tsp. Tabasco sauce
2 oz. horseradish
3 oz. chili sauce
3 oz. ketchup

Mix together. For shrimp cocktail, add shrimp and let stand in refrigerator an hour or more. Or serve as a dip for shrimp.

Quick and Easy Vegetable Dips

A

1 pkg. italian dressing mix (dry)
1 pint sour cream
¼ tsp. curry powder

Simply stir together and store in refrigerator.

B

1 c. mayonnaise
½ c. sour cream
1 clove garlic, crushed
1 small onion, finely chopped
1 green onion, finely chopped
Dash salt, celery salt, garlic salt
    and worcestershire sauce

Mix all ingredients well.

Adjust seasonings to your own taste.

Store in jar in refrigerator.

Sweet and Sour Sauce

¾ c. brown sugar
¼ c. soya sauce
⅓ c. vinegar
⅔ c. water
2 tbsp. ketchup
3 tbsp. cornstarch dissolved in ¼ c. water

Bring this to a boil.

Store in refrigerator for future use.

Heat to serve as a dip with our sausage balls, or spoon over a meat loaf before baking. A hit with your kids!

Barbecue Sauce

1 can (10 oz.) tomato soup
½ c. brown sugar
½ c. vinegar
½ tsp. paprika
1 tsp. celery salt
1 tsp. chili powder
½ tsp. ground cloves
Dash salt

Stir together all ingredients and heat.

An excellent sauce for ribs, tails, chicken, chops, etc.

Toppings for Cream Cheese

A

1 jar (8 oz.) pineapple jam
1 jar (8 oz.) apple jelly
1 tbsp. dry mustard
2-½ oz. horseradish

Just mix together and store in the same jam and jelly jars in refrigerator. May be kept for months.

Spoon over a bar of cream cheese and serve with crackers.

B

1 pkg. (8 oz.) cream cheese
1 tbsp. soya sauce

Place cream cheese in small serving dish. Prick with a fork.

Marinate in soya sauce for a few hours.

Delicious spread on melba toast or crackers.

May also be sprinkled with toasted almonds or toasted sesame seeds.

Dips for Fruit

Chocolate Dip
3 oz. whipping cream
3 squares semi-sweet chocolate
2 tsp. Grand Marnier

Pour whipping cream in saucepan.

Add chocolate and stir until creamy at low heat.

Add Grand Marnier.

For dipping bananas, maraschino cherries with stems, apples or pears.

Crème Fraîche
1 c. whipping cream
½ c. sour cream
Grated peel of 1 lemon
4 tsp. lemon juice
2 tsp. white sugar

In small bowl, mix whipping cream and sour cream until smooth.

Cover and let stand at room temperature until thick (about 24 hrs.).

Stir in lemon peel, lemon juice and sugar.

Cover and refrigerate. Will keep for at least 3 days.

Makes 1-½ cups.

Dips for Fruit

Cream Cheese Dip
1 pkg. (8 oz.) cream cheese, softened
1 c. frozen strawberries, slightly thawed

Put in blender and blend until smooth.

Add more strawberries for a pinker colour, if desired.

A little sugar may be added for a sweeter taste.

Delicious for bananas, pineapple, apple, grapes–all fresh fruit.

Sour Cream Dip

1 c. sour cream
2 tbsp. dark brown sugar

Mix together. Spoon into bowl and sprinkle with small
amount of brown sugar.

Hooked on Seafood

Crab Meat Appetizers

---

1 pkg. (8 oz.) refrigerator butterflake rolls
1 can (7 oz.) crab meat, drained and flaked
¼ c. minced celery
½ tsp. salt
½ tsp. dry mustard
Dash Tabasco sauce
Dash worcestershire sauce
¼ c. sour cream
2 tbsp. mayonnaise
¼ c. shredded cheddar cheese (or more)

Divide each biscuit in half. Press into small muffin cups.

Mix all remaining ingredients except cheese.

Place about one tablespoon of filling in each shell. Top with a sprinkle of cheese.

Bake at 350° F for 15 min. or until cheese is melted.

Cool and freeze.

Makes 20 appetizers.

Crab Swiss Bites

1 can (7 oz.) crab meat, drained and flaked
1 c. (4 oz.) grated swiss cheese
½ c. mayonnaise
1 tbsp. chopped onion
1 tsp. lemon juice
½ tsp. salt
¼ tsp. curry powder
1 pkg. (8 oz.) refrigerator butterflake rolls

Combine all ingredients except rolls.

Separate each roll into three and place on ungreased cookie sheet.

Spoon crab mixture on biscuits.

Bake at 350° F for 10 min.

Try putting a slice of water chestnut on top of crab mixture before baking.

Donna's Shrimp Mousse

1 envelope unflavoured gelatin
¼ c. cold water
1 pkg. (8 oz.) cream cheese
1 can (10 oz.) tomato soup
1 c. mayonnaise
2 cans small shrimp (7 oz. each),
    drained and cut into pieces
½ c. finely chopped onion
1 green pepper, finely chopped

Soften gelatin in cold water.

Put cream cheese and soup in double boiler and heat, stirring until well blended. (Beat with beaters if it isn't smooth enough.)

Stir gelatin and mayonnaise into soup mixture.

Let cool slightly, then stir in shrimp (reserving a few for garnish), onion and green pepper.

Pour into oiled 4-cup mold or individual molds and chill.

Unmold and garnish with parsley and shrimp. Serve with assorted crackers.

May be stored in refrigerator for a couple of days or may be frozen.

Hot Crab and Cheese Dip

---

1 pkg. (8 oz.) cream cheese, softened
1 can (7 oz.) crab meat, drained and flaked
Worcestershire sauce to taste (½–1 tsp.)
Tabasco sauce to taste (couple of drops)
1 tbsp. sour cream
1 tbsp. lemon juice or vinegar
¼ tsp. salt
Grated parmesan cheese

Mix all ingredients except parmesan cheese together.

Sprinkle parmesan on top.

Put in oven-proof dish, one that may be taken to the table, and bake at 350° F for ½ hr.

Great for cracker-dipping.

For those who can't eat seafood, substitute flakes of ham or corned beef for the crab–it's just as good!

Louise's Crab Stuffed Snow Peas

⅓ lb. fresh snow peas (30–36 pods)
1 can (7 oz.) crab meat, drained and flaked
1 tbsp. mayonnaise
Salt and pepper
1 tbsp. chili sauce or seafood sauce
Dash Tabasco sauce

Steam peas for 1 min. (no longer, as they should be a bright green).

Rinse in cold water and drain.

Mix the rest of the ingredients together.

Carefully open pods and stuff with crab mixture.

Chill.

Variation:

Stuff with 4 oz. softened cream cheese mixed with 1 tbsp. parsley, ½ tsp. dried basil and 1 tsp. lemon juice.

A gourmet treat for crab lovers, and an attractive addition to your nibble tray.

Pat Scott's Lobster Roll

¼ lb. butter
½ lb. Velveeta cheese
2 cans (7 oz. each) lobster or crab,
    drained and flaked
1 large loaf sliced bread
Butter, melted

Melt butter and cheese and add lobster or crab.

Trim crusts from bread, roll until thin and spread each slice with mixture. Roll up, wrap in foil and freeze.

To serve, slice rolls in half rounds, dip in melted butter, bake on cookie sheet 10–12 min. in 350° F oven.

Makes 40 snacks.

Dee's Crab Meat Appetizers

1 can (7 oz.) crab meat, drained and flaked
1 scant cup processed cheese
1 tsp. worcestershire sauce
¼ tsp. pepper
½ tsp. onion powder
1 egg yolk
1 pkg. frozen cocktail vol-au-vent (patty shells)

Combine filling ingredients and fill shells. Freeze.
When ready to use, bake 10 min. at 400° F.

Salmon Dip

---

    1 pkg. (4 oz.) cream cheese, softened
    1 c. sour cream
    2 tbsp. mayonnaise
    1 tsp. lemon juice
    ½ tsp. grated lemon peel
    2 tbsp. finely chopped celery
    2 tbsp. finely chopped green onion
    1 can (7-¾ oz.) salmon, drained
    Salt and freshly ground pepper

Blend together cream cheese, sour cream, mayonnaise, lemon juice and peel.

Stir in remaining ingredients, seasoning to taste with salt and pepper.

Chill.

Makes about 2 cups.

Shrimp Dip

¾ c. small shrimp, drained
½ c. chili sauce
3 tbsp. tomato paste
2 tbsp. lemon juice
1 pkg. (8 oz.) cream cheese, softened
1 tbsp. horseradish
¼ c. chopped dill pickles

Mix ingredients together.

Makes 2 cups.

May be frozen.

Tastes like a shrimp cocktail when served with crackers.

Salmon Log

1 can (16 oz.) red salmon
1 pkg. (8 oz.) cream cheese, softened
1 tbsp. lemon juice
2 tsp. grated onion
1 tsp. horseradish
¼ tsp. liquid smoke
½ c. chopped pecans
3 tbsp. chopped parsley or parsley flakes

Drain and flake salmon, removing skin and bones.

Combine all other ingredients except nuts and parsley.

Chill several hours.

Mix chopped pecans and parsley. Shape salmon mixture into log and roll in nut-parsley mixture and refrigerate.

May be frozen.

It is hard to find liquid smoke, but we can usually find it in a cheese specialty store. Share the bottle with friends, as a little goes a long way.

Salmon Mousse

1 can (7-¾ oz.) salmon
1 tbsp. unflavoured gelatin
¾ c. salad dressing or mayonnaise
½ c. chopped celery or green pepper
¼ c. chopped olives
1 tbsp. lemon juice
Salt and pepper to taste

Drain salmon, reserving liquid. Add cold water to liquid until volume reaches ¼ cup.

Sprinkle gelatin over liquid, and place over low heat until dissolved.

Add to dressing.

Fold in salmon, celery, olives and seasoning.

Place in small individual molds for your hors-d'oeuvres tray, or in your seafood mold for your buffet table.

Sardine Pâté

---

2 cans (3-½ oz. each) sardines
6 tbsp. butter, softened
2 tbsp. cream cheese, softened
1 tbsp. lemon juice
1 tbsp. worcestershire sauce
1 tsp. ketchup
Dash garlic powder
¼ tsp. salt
⅛ tsp. cayenne

Mash sardines. Mix with the butter and cheese and blend to a smooth paste.

Season with lemon juice, worcestershire, ketchup, garlic, salt and cayenne.

Refrigerate.

Makes 1 cup.

Tuna Cups

1 small can (7 oz.) tuna
1 hardboiled egg, chopped
1 c. (4 oz.) shredded cheddar cheese
⅓ c. chopped celery
¼ c. mayonnaise
1 pkg. (8 oz.) refrigerator butterflake rolls

Combine tuna, egg, cheese, celery and mayonnaise. Mix well.

Separate butterflake rolls and divide each one in two.
Press into bottom and up sides of ungreased muffin cups.

Spoon tuna mixture into cups.

Bake at 350° F for 10–15 min.

Makes 20.

Our tasters thought these were delicious and a nice change from the richness of shell fish.

ABOUT THE AUTHORS

S ISTERS Joan Pauli and Cathy Prange grew up in Ontario with the enticing smell of homemade muffins in their mother's kitchen. As a result, the two learned the basics of muffinery at an early age. Each later married, had three children and began honing her skills in muffin creation. It was in 1982 when the sisters started baking an incredibly wide variety of creative, scrumptious muffins on a regular basis. Family and friends devoured Cathy and Joan's diverse muffinery as soon as the treats left the ovens. At the same time, they urged Prange and Pauli to share recipes for their creations. Muffin Mania became an instant sensation in Canada.

Cathy Prange and Joan Pauli worked tirelessly at marketing, selling and promoting *Muffin Mania* throughout Canada. The sisters authored *Nibble Mania* (formerly *Nifty Nibbles*), a collection of appetizers, finger foods and snacks, that followed quickly on the heels of *Muffin Mania*'s success.

Veggie Mania, consisting of easy-to-prepare soups, salads and veggie casseroles, was published in 1986. Encouraged by their success and numerous requests for "what's next?" they compiled their favourite recipes for sweet lovers, and *Sweet Mania* was launched. This delightful book contains recipes for delicious pies, cakes, mouth-watering desserts, cookies and squares and a selection of their Christmas goodies.